Corn – On and Off the Cob

By Allan Fowler

Consultants
Robert L. Hillerich, Professor Emeritus,
Bowling Green State University, Bowling Green, Ohio;
Consultant, Pinellas County Schools, Florida

Lynne Kepler, Educational Consultant

Fay Robinson, Child Development Specialist

CHILDRENS PRESS®

CHICAGO

Design by Beth Herman Design Associates
Photo Research by Feldman & Associates, Inc.

Library of Congress Cataloging-in-Publication Data

Fowler, Allan.
    Corn — On and Off the Cob / by Allan Fowler.
      p. cm. – (Rookie read-about science)
    ISBN 0-516-06027-9
    1. Corn–Juvenile literature. [1. Corn.]
  I. Title. II. Series.
SB191.MsF657   1994
633.1'5–dc20   94-10471
                                         CIP
                                         AC

What food is grown on
more American farms
than any other?

Apples? No.
Potatoes? No.
Corn? Yes!

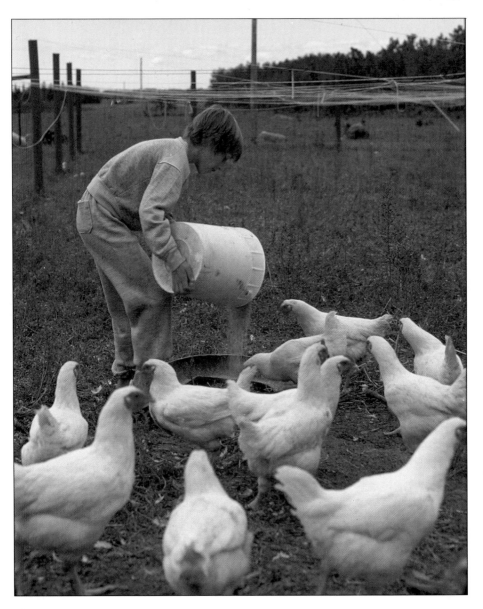

Most of that corn is not eaten by people.

Farm animals eat a lot of corn.

The corn that hogs, cattle, and poultry eat is called field corn.

The kind that you eat
is sweet corn.

Corn on the cob, fresh
from the farm, is one
way to enjoy it.

But kernels are also taken
off the cob. They are
canned or frozen, so you
can have corn any time
of the year.

One special kind of corn
pops when you heat it.
I'm sure you know what
that kind is called!

There are many other ways
to eat corn.

You might eat succotash.
That is a mixture of corn
and lima beans.

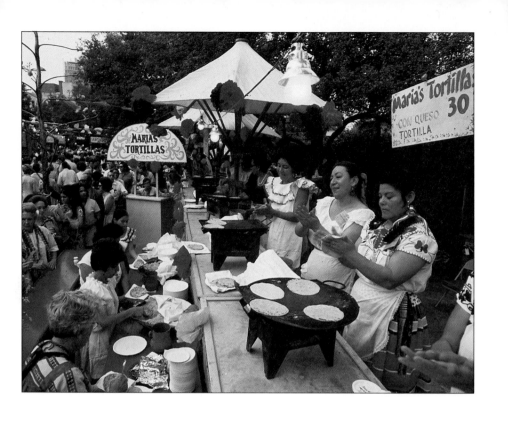

Corn is ground into
cornmeal, which is used to
make corn bread and corn
muffins, tacos and tortillas.

And don't forget cornflakes.

You often eat corn without knowing it. Jam and jelly, candy and soda pop may contain corn syrup or corn sugar.

If these foods make your
fingers sticky, you may
wash your hands with
soap that contains corn oil.

American Indians were
the first people to raise
corn. They called it
maize. We often call
it Indian corn.

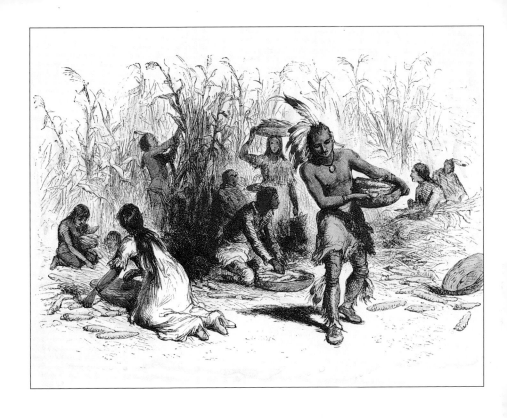

The Indians taught
the Pilgrims and other
settlers from Europe
how to grow corn.

Corn plants belong to the same family of plants as grass.

Grasses that are used for food — corn and rice, oats and barley, wheat and buckwheat — are known as cereal grains.

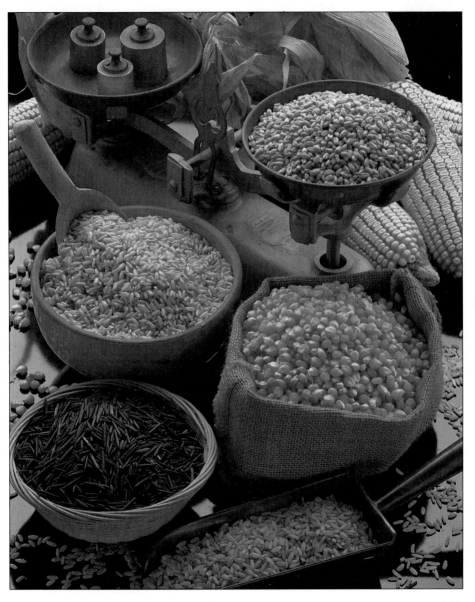

A cornstalk usually grows to be at least 7 feet tall. Cornstalks in some places might grow as tall as 20 feet.

On top of each stalk is a tassel. One, or sometimes two, ears of corn grow on each stalk.

The ears are covered by husks. Under the husks are cobs. The cobs are covered with row after row of kernels.

The silky threads on the ears of corn are called corn silk.

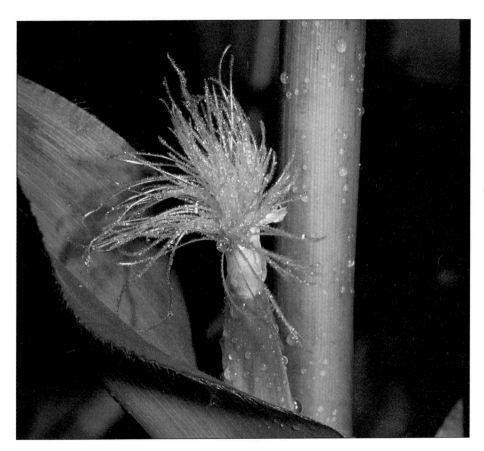

Most of the corn we eat
has yellow kernels.

But corn can also be
white, red, brown, purple
— or even have different
colors on the same cob.

Farm families used to
gather for a party while
removing the husks from
the ears. They called these
parties husking bees.

Today, machines are used to plant, harvest, and husk corn. Machines make it even easier to grow and enjoy corn.

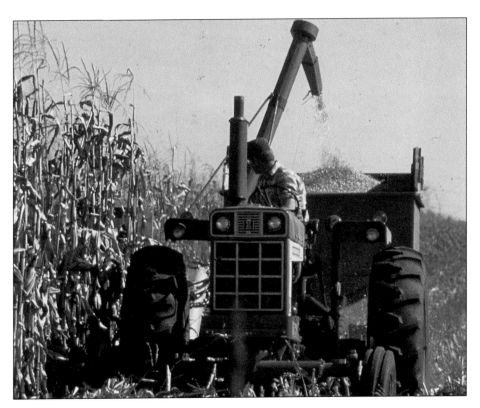

Corn on the cob, popcorn, creamed corn, cornflakes, tortillas, tacos . . .

What is your favorite way to eat corn?

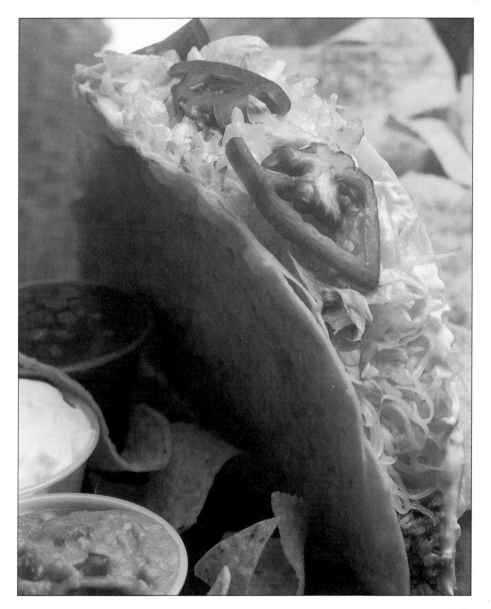

Words You Know

corn

cornstalk

Indian corn (maize)

popcorn

corn on the cob

30

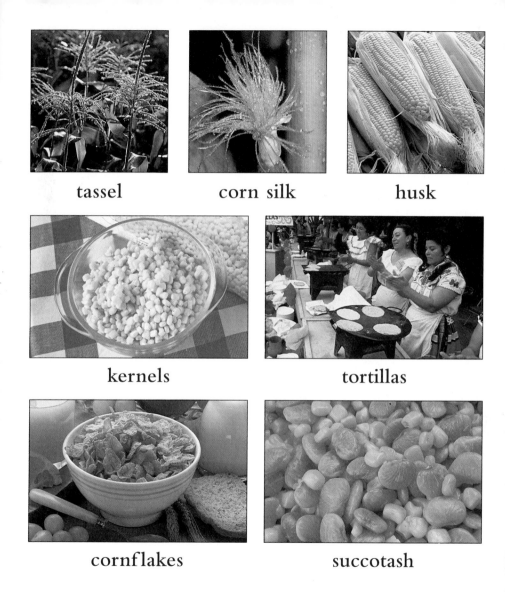

tassel   corn silk   husk

kernels   tortillas

cornflakes   succotash

31

Index

American Indians, 16, 17
apples, 3
barley, 18
buckwheat, 18
candy, 14
canned corn, 8
cereal grains, 18
colors of corn, 24, 25
corn bread, 12
corncobs, 8, 22, 25
cornflakes, 13, 28, 31
corn husks, 22, 26, 31
corn kernels, 8, 22, 24, 31
cornmeal, 12
corn muffins, 12
corn oil, 15
corn on the cob, 6, 28, 30
corn plants, 18
corn silk, 23, 31
cornstalks, 20, 21, 30
corn sugar, 14
corn syrup, 14
corn tassels, 21, 31
creamed corn, 28
ears of corn, 21, 22, 23, 26
farm animals, 5

farms, 3, 6
field corn, 5
frozen corn, 8
grass, 18
harvesting corn, 27
husking bees, 26
husking corn, 27
Indian corn, 16, 30
jam, 14
jelly, 14
lima beans, 10
maize, 16, 30
oats, 18
Pilgrims, 17
planting corn, 27
popcorn, 9, 28, 30
potatoes, 3
rice, 18
soap, 15
soda pop, 14
succotash, 10, 31
sweet corn, 6
tacos, 12, 28
tortillas, 12, 28, 31
wheat, 18

About the Author

Allan Fowler is a free-lance writer with a background in advertising. Born in New York, he lives in Chicago now and enjoys traveling.

Photo Credits

North Wind Picture Archives – 17, 26

PhotoEdit – © David Young-Wolff, 8, 11, 15, 24, 30 (bottom right), 31 (center left and bottom right); ©Paul Conklin, 27

Tom Stack & Associates – ©Gerald & Buff Corsi, 23, 31 (top center)

Tony Stone Images – ©Brian Seed, 12, 31 (center right)

SuperStock International, Inc. – Cover, 13, 19, 25, 30 (top right), 31 (bottom left); ©Kro/SuperStock, 7; ©Micheal Rutherford, 9, 30 (bottom left); ©Mick Roessler, 20, 30 (top left); ©Fletcher Collection, 21, 31 (top left), ©Richard Heinzen, 29

Valan – ©Wayne Shiels, 4; ©Kennon Cooke, 14, 22, 31 (top right)

COVER: Corn